362.82
Hig

DISCARDED

Bedford Free Public Library
Bedford, Massachusetts 01730

Home of the Bedford Flag

The Bedford Flag, commissioned to Cornet John Page in 1737 by King George II of England, was carried by his son, Nathaniel, who fought with the Bedford Minutemen at the Battle of Concord Bridge, April 19, 1775.

FEB 2012

Life's Challenges

The Night Dad Went to Jail

What to Expect When Someone You Love Goes to Jail

by Melissa Higgins

illustrated by Wednesday Kirwan

PICTURE WINDOW BOOKS
a capstone imprint

This is one of my *before* drawings. *Before* means "before my dad went to jail." Dad and I didn't catch anything, but we had fun anyway.

My dad calls me Sketch because I like to draw. Miss Sanchez, my school counselor, says drawing is a good way for me to show my feelings. I must have a lot of feelings. I draw all the time!

We were at Dad's apartment the night the police came. Lights flashed. Neighbors stared. The officers put my dad in handcuffs. Jasmine and TJ started crying.

One of the officers walked over to us. I thought he was going to arrest us too! But he smiled and handed TJ a teddy bear.

"Where are you taking my dad?" I asked. **"What did he do?"**

"Your dad may have broken a law," the officer said. **"We need to ask him some questions at the police station."**

Laws are rules that tell people how they should behave. When people break a law, they may be put in jail or prison. They have to stay there for a period of time. How long depends upon what law they broke.

The officer stayed until a social worker came. Her name was Mrs. Garvin. She asked if I had any questions about what was going on. Was I scared? Did I want a glass of water?

She was nice, but I just shook my head.
I was happy when Mom came to pick us up.

Mom talked on the phone almost all night. Before tucking me in, she told me Dad admitted he broke a law. He was in trouble. And he would have to stay in jail for a while.

I asked Mom if it was my fault. She said it wasn't. Dad just made a bad choice. She said no matter what, she and Dad would always love me.

My stomach didn't feel so woozy after that. But why had Dad done it? He'd left us! I thought about drawing. But I was too sad to draw.

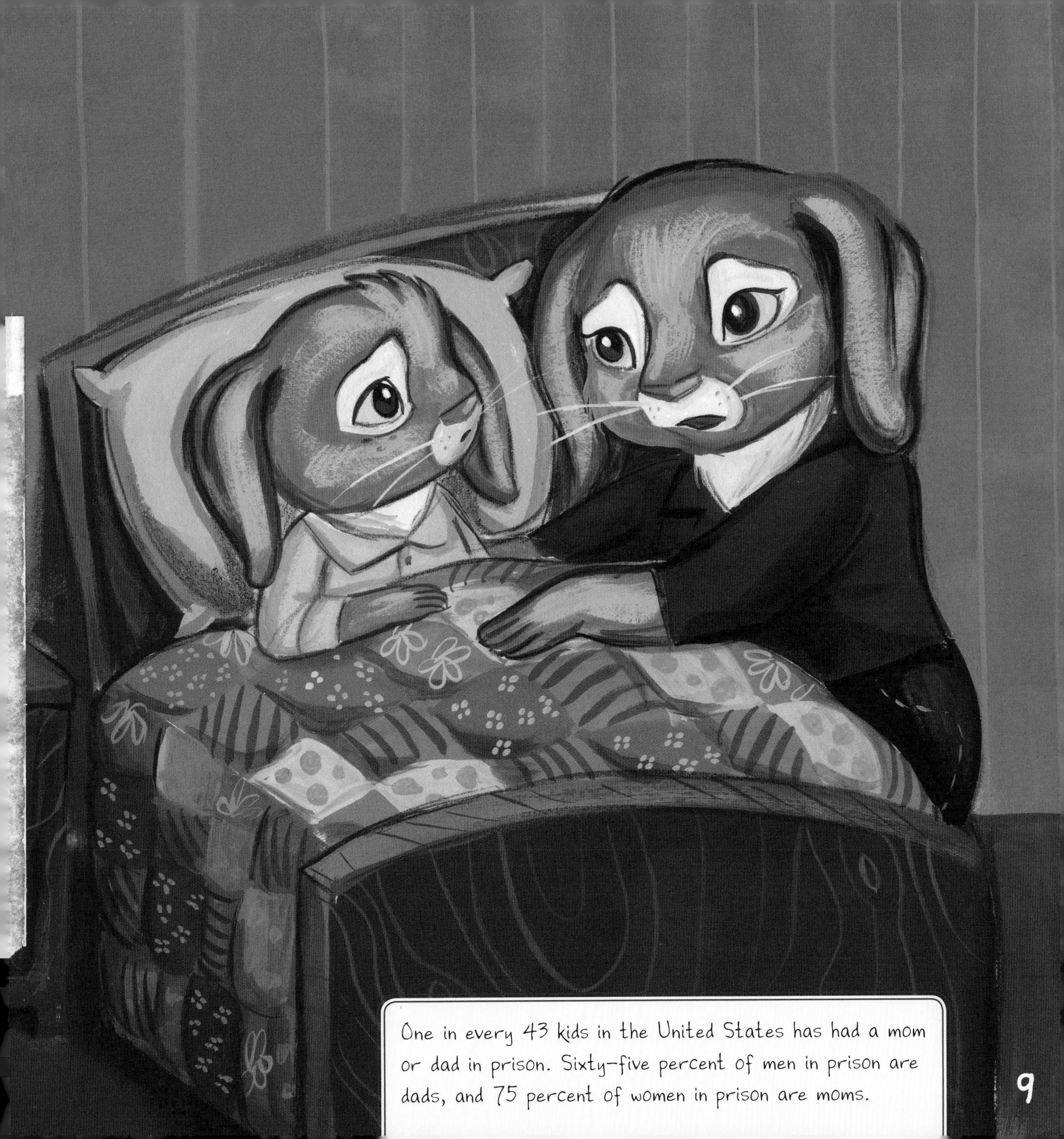

One in every 43 kids in the United States has had a mom or dad in prison. Sixty-five percent of men in prison are dads, and 75 percent of women in prison are moms.

The next morning, I kept my head down. I tried to hide behind my books. But Kenny saw me. Kenny lives on Dad's street. He saw Dad get into the police car.

"Bailey's dad got picked up by the cops last night!" Kenny yelled.

My face got hot. I crept into class, wishing I could erase myself.

Later, Mr. Johnson asked me a question. I didn't even hear him.

Ava poked me in the back.
"Hey! Wake up, jailbird!"

I got so mad, I twisted around and pushed her books onto the floor.

That's how I ended up in Miss Sanchez's office.

I'd never been in trouble before. Miss Sanchez had called my mom and found out what happened to Dad. I sat and scribbled.

"Is that a picture of you?" she asked, looking at the paper.

"I guess," I said. **"I don't know. Everything's all messed up."**

Miss Sanchez said feeling angry, sad, and scared was OK. So was feeling worried and embarrassed. She gave me ideas for what to do with my "scribble" feelings. Next time, I can walk away instead of fighting. I can draw pictures or talk to someone I trust.

For a while, Dad was in jail nearby. Mom visited first and told us what it was like. When we all went, we took the bus. Dad sat on the other side of a glass wall. We each talked to him on a telephone. When it was my turn, I couldn't look at him.

"I messed up, Sketch," Dad said. "What I did caused a lot of problems, and I'm sorry. I hope you'll forgive me."

I wasn't sure what to say. I just nodded.

Lots of kids don't know what to say to their parent in jail or prison. Talking about school and everyday life is a great place to start.

After four months, Dad was sent to a prison farther away. Our bus ride took all morning. Once we got there, we walked through a metal detector. The prison was really scary, but we could visit Dad without a wall between us.

It's common to feel excited, nervous, and restless before and after visiting a parent in jail or prison.

Hugging him was one of the best feelings I'd had in a long time.

We see Dad about once a month. In between visits, I send him drawings, and he writes me letters. Sometimes we talk on the phone.

Miss Sanchez found a group of other kids who have a mom or dad in prison. We get together every Tuesday. They're cool. They understand what I'm going through.

Things have changed since Dad went to prison. Mom works even more than she used to. Grandma helps take care of us now. Mrs. Garvin, the social worker, found me a mentor too. He's not my dad, but it's nice having someone to hang out with.

Staying in touch with a parent in jail or prison helps kids get used to being apart. And it helps Dad or Mom feel more like a part of the family when he or she returns.

Dad's sentence is for six years. That's a long time to wait to go fishing again. I'm still a little angry. But I'm working on forgiving my dad, because I love him.

Glossary

arrest—to take and hold someone who may have broken a law

jail—an enclosed space where people are taken when they are first arrested and where they may serve a sentence of a year or less

mentor—a person who guides or teaches

prison—an enclosed space where people are sent after they've been found guilty of a crime and must serve a year or more

sentence—the amount of time a person is required by the court to stay in a jail or prison

social worker—a person trained to help people during times of trouble

Read More

Brisson, Pat. *Mama Loves Me from Away.* Honesdale, Penn.: Boyds Mills Press, 2004.

Williams, Vera B. *Amber Was Brave, Essie Was Smart: The Story of Amber and Essie Told Here in Poems and Pictures.* New York: Greenwillow Books, 2001.

Woodson, Jacqueline. *Visiting Day.* New York: Scholastic Press, 2002.

Internet Sites

FactHound offers a safe, fun way to find Internet sites related to this book. All of the sites on FactHound have been researched by our staff.

Here's all you do:

Visit *www.facthound.com*

Type in this code: 9781404866799

WWW.FACTHOUND.COM®

Check out projects, games and lots more at **www.capstonekids.com**

Index

Look for all the books in the Life's Challenges series:

Good-bye, Jeepers

The Night Dad Went to Jail

Saying Good-bye to Uncle Joe

Weekends with Dad

Thanks to our advisers for their expertise, research, and advice:

Michele Goyette-Ewing, PhD
Director of Psychology Training
Yale Child Study Center

Terry Flaherty, PhD
Professor of English
Minnesota State University, Mankato

Editor: Jill Kalz
Designer: Alison Thiele
Art Director: Nathan Gassman
Production Specialist: Sarah Bennett
The illustrations in this book were created with gouache and colored pencil.

Picture Window Books
151 Good Counsel Drive
P.O. Box 669
Mankato, MN 56002-0669
877-845-8392
www.capstonepub.com

Copyright © 2012 by Picture Window Books, a Capstone imprint.
All rights reserved. No part of this book may be reproduced without written permission from the publisher. The publisher takes no responsibility for the use of any of the materials or methods described in this book, nor for the products thereof.

All books published by Picture Window Books are manufactured with paper containing at least 10 percent post-consumer waste.

Library of Congress Cataloging-in-Publication Data
Higgins, Melissa, 1953–
The night dad went to jail : what to expect when someone you love goes to jail / by Melissa Higgins ; illustrated by Wednesday Kirwan.
p. cm. — (Life's challenges)
ISBN 978-1-4048-6679-9 (library binding)
1. Children of prisoners—United States. 2. Prisoners—Family relationships—United States. 3. Prisons—United States—Juvenile literature. 4. Father and child—United States. I. Kirwan, Wednesday. II. Title. III. Series.

HV8886.U5H54 2012
362.82'950973—dc22 2011007456

Printed in the United States of America in North Mankato, Minnesota.
032011 006110CGF11